Exploring a Theme: Religon Around me

Exploring religion ar
– listening to childr

Religion around me – what does this mean? Where do we look to find 'religion' in our local community? Do we just mean identifying and finding out about local places of worship? This is a good starting point, and an important part of any RE curriculum, but religion is more than this. Religion concerns people – it is about **believing, worshipping, valuing**; it is about **belonging** to a faith community and **living** within the wider community. Helping children to explore this wider concept of religion means engaging with believers and helping pupils to listen and talk to people of faith.

This publication provides ideas and resources to help you do this. In the section for 4–6 year olds, we hear how one teacher uses a visit to a church to get children talking about their puzzling questions. The 5–7 year olds section focuses on what it is like to belong to a faith community, suggesting classroom activities to explore what 'belonging' to a religion means for one family at a special time in the year.

The visual learning activity on the centre pages provides a resource which can be used in a variety of ways at different levels. It aims to get pupils thinking and talking about the many ways religion and belief affect everyday life in Britain today

Another way of helping pupils 'encounter' people from other faiths is through listening to their 'story'. In the interviews on pages 18 onwards, children from a range of religions speak, not as representatives of their faiths, but as individuals. These interviews provide a glimpse of their faith, as they understand it, at a particular moment of time. The activities provided with each interview aim to help you make the most of these 'insights' to engage pupils with the issues and questions raised. Try using the questions in the interviews with children in your own school (downloadable from our website at www.retoday.org.uk for RE Today subscribers). Celebrate the beliefs and insights of children in your own community.

Joyce Mackley
Editor

RE Today weblink: www.retoday.org.uk

The RE Today website provides some free additional resources and classroom ready materials for subscibers. Look out for the 'RE Today on the web' logo at the end of selected articles.

The password for access can be found in each term's *REtoday* magazine.

Focus	Title	Page No.
4–6	Visiting a local church – engaging children's 'puzzling questions' Paul Newbould, Minchinhampton Primary School, Gloucestershire	2
5–7	What does it mean to belong to a Christian family at Christmas? Denise Brogden, RE Today	8
7–11	Religion around us: a visual learning activity Joyce Mackley, RE Today	14
7–11	Meet Nathan (Roman Catholic) Anna Nugent, Wellington Primary School, Herefordshire	18
7–11	Meet Dora (Quaker) Peter Fishpool and Rosemary Rivett, RE Today	20
7–11	Meet Alice (Buddhist) Lat Blaylock, RE Today	22
7–11	Meet Rohit (Hindu) Phil Albans and Denise Brogden, RE Today	24
7–11	Meet Yahya (Muslim) Joyce Mackley, RE Today	26
7–11	Meet Samuel (Jewish) Anne Krisman and Rosemary Rivett, RE Today	28
7–11	Meet Eeshar (Sikh) Roop Singh and Pamela Draycott, RE Today	30
7–11	Meet Kian (Bahai) Midge Ault, Leominster Junior School, Herefordshire, and Joyce Mackley, RE Today	32

Visiting a local church – engaging children's 'puzzling questions'

For the teacher

How can we make a church visit valuable and meaningful for younger pupils?

One way is to use a class teddy to pose puzzling questions and to motivate pupils to ask their own.

This 'puzzled teddy' approach has at its heart an ethos which values pupils' talk.

This article suggests practical strategies to value, focus and harness pupils' talk to enable younger pupils to make sense of a church visit.

I can ...

The following pupil-friendly criteria could be used to assess children's responses to the activities.

Level 1 describes what most 6-year-olds should be able to do.

Level 1 – I can ...

- remember and tell someone about three things I know Christians use in their worship in church
- recognise a symbol special to Christians, from inside a church, and talk about an interesting or puzzling question I'd like to know about it.

Level 2 – I can ...

- identify three Christian symbols from my visit to a church, and link one of them to a story from the Bible
- suggest three questions about God or Jesus that are interesting or hard to answer, following my visit to a church.

Foundation Stage links to Personal, Social, Emotional Development

These activities encourage children to respond, showing a range of feelings. They develop understanding that people have different cultures and beliefs, which need to be treated with respect.

In this section Paul Newbould, teacher at Minchinhampton Primary School in Gloucestershire, shares his class activities on a common aspect of RE.

First some reflections from Paul on how he came to try this approach in his RE teaching:

I had begun to realise that asking children to simply label the parts of a church fails to connect them with what a church really means to the Christians who worship there.

So what does make a connection? 'Symbol and story' came to mind in that they together reflect something of the relationship Christians have with Jesus. Behind the symbols and images in traditional church buildings we can see the key stories of the Christian faith.

So perhaps our goal should be to make links with children's emerging, if fragmentary, understanding of the Jesus stories of Easter and Christmas.

But how? I had read Margaret Donaldson's view that pupils can move beyond the confines of Piaget's stage theory if the context has relevance for them; she cites McGarrigle's 'naughty teddy' experiment (Margaret Donaldson, *Children's Minds,* Harper Perennial 1978, p.64).

I had also learned of recent work in RE using Persona Dolls and was keen to try something akin to this approach with our 'class teddy'.

Perhaps our puzzled teddy could provide a 'way in' to the topic.

Visiting a church

Visiting a local church – activities before the visit

4–6

For the teacher
Take photos of Teddy 'visiting' the church
- Find all the light switches and use a tripod if possible to avoid blurring from camera shake, as flash will not carry far.
- Select images to photograph which carry religious meaning for them, such as cross, pulpit, stained-glass window and altar, avoiding nave, pillar and aisle!

Build the slideshow and script
- Build a PowerPoint or simple slideshow showing Teddy's visit.
- Plan your script, introducing the symbols without naming them at this stage, showing how much they puzzle Teddy.

Book of Teddy's visit
- Compile a class book from the slideshow pictures, as an ongoing resource for pupils to 'read' and talk about.

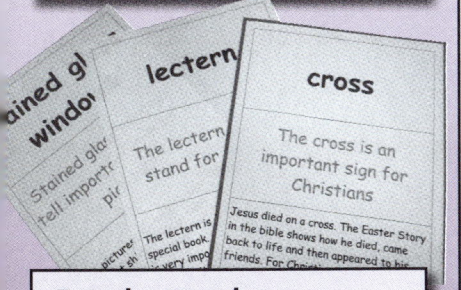

For the teacher
Prepare photos and captions for pupils to handle:
- Laminate photos of Teddy's visit.
- Print key words and meanings onto card, allowing differentiation for readers: an enlarged key word, then a simple sentence, then a detailed paragraph.

Getting started activity: Teddy tells his story
Teddy's story of his visit, with PowerPoint
- Explain to class how puzzled Teddy was by this building he had seen (nearby/ in town). He decided to go and explore it, but a lot of things puzzled him there.
- Devise a script to tell children 'Teddy's story', leaving opportunities for them to engage with what is 'puzzling teddy', e.g. *'What a big place, a lot of people could fit in here! Look at that bright window, with a baby, a very special baby, in the middle...I wonder why are they bringing him presents?'* etc.

Pupil talk at this stage
- Allow the pupils to offer meanings or key words if they know them, but otherwise let Teddy tell the story in his own puzzled way.
- This is important. It shows pupils that it is OK to be puzzled!

Vocabulary-building activity:
Whole class:
- Shared reading of key words and captions
- Recall how puzzled Teddy was. Are you puzzled by these words or pictures?
- Explain that the class will be visiting the church soon and they first need to learn the names that Christians use for features of the church.

Matching task in groups:
- Can you match the pictures to the correct key word and meaning? Talk as you go, including questions.

Whole class:
- Ask pupils to use their new vocabulary to describe or explain the pictures.
- Ask 'What still puzzles you about particular pictures or key words?' Record questions in big bubbles.

Visiting a local church: activities during the visit

Visit-planning tips for the teacher

- **Structure small groups:** it helps if children can talk in a focused way within small 'family' groups of 3–5, supported by an adult (parent/teaching assistant).
- **Scaffold the talk:** a well-designed talk record sheet (see page 6), will help support both adults and children to stay on task and keep the talk options quite open.
- **Plan for reflection:** young pupils will not easily linger and reflect, so a sketching task will enable children to stay long enough at each feature and allow time for other adults to scribe their talk.
- **Brief other adults:** save time and confusion on the day by planning in time beforehand to talk through the roles and strategies for the visit.

Activities within the church

- **Whole class – Recognising key features:** link with Teddy's pictures and ask the class, while seated in the nave, which parts they can recognise. The class can be briefed on the following tasks while sitting.
- **Group task – Sketching and responding:** while the group focuses on a key feature or symbol, the adult helper can prompt and record their thoughts and questions using the recording sheets on pages 6 and 7. Groups can then rotate. Not all parts need be 'done' by all, since reporting back later is an important talking and sharing opportunity.
- **Whole class option – mini worship:** this can be brought more to life, if time permits, by taking part in a short class assembly in the church. Plan beforehand with your class, by choosing a familiar song, prayer and Bible story, and make use of the pulpit and the lectern to model the Sunday experience.

Visiting a church

Visiting a local church: activities during the visit

4-6

Group task – Guided reflection
- Use the cards on page 7.
- Visit each group in turn to review and extend their scribed responses.
- Back in school they may be more responsive and able to think more clearly, without the 'distraction' of the visit.
- Groups can also complete any part-finished sketches, using Teddy's visit photos to complete any missing details.

Thoughts and Feelings

> It feeled nice . . . because it was Jesus home

> Everyone is happy at this church. I felt cheerful.

> I felt sad and angry that Jesus died.

> I thought about Jesus dying on the cross.

Symbols and Stories

> I felt sorry for Jesus that he had to die, and he must have been terrified.

> They killed him 'cos they were jealous. Christians believe in Jesus and Jesus is here.

> Jesus came back to life and Mary came running to tell her friends.

For the teacher – Collating questions and thoughts
- Collate all the completed group record sheets.
- Group and prioritise them according to the expectations of the unit.
- Re-scribe key quotes on individual A4-plus bubbles.
- Sequence the bubble sheets for the Shared enquiry.

Whole class – Shared enquiry

Use a 'think – pair – share' approach to 'process' the selected quotes. Take the 'smaller' or more closed questions first. This may need more than one lesson. One way to group the quotes is shown here:

- **Thoughts and Feelings:** a chance to look at diversity and respecting others' views.
- **Symbols and Stories:** link key symbols with a familiar Bible story to extend children's understanding.
- **Puzzling Questions:** what is the biggest question of all, which we may not be able to answer today?

Puzzling Questions

> Why did the nasty people kill Jesus?

> Why are there so many crosses of Jesus dying in the church?

5

REtoday Services

Questions we want to ask
- while sitting inside the Parish Church
- after visiting the Parish Church

Thousands of people may have talked to God in this church.
- What questions do you think people might have asked God in their prayers?
- Do you have a question about this church?
- Do you have a question you want to ask God?
- What do you think God is saying in answer?

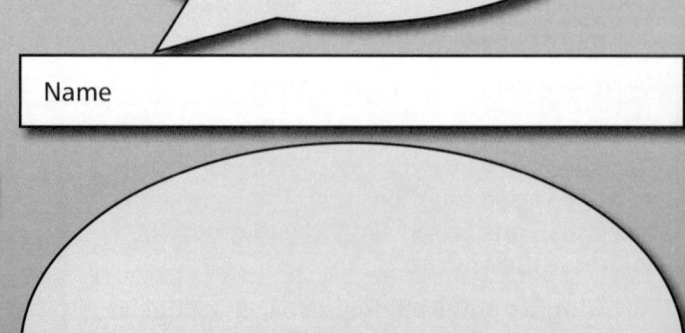

Name

Name

Name

Name

Name

Name

Name

© 2007 RE Today Services
Permission is granted to photocopy this page for use in classroom activities in schools that have purchased this publication.

Visiting a church

4-6

Thoughts we have had
- while sitting inside the Parish Church
- after visiting the Parish Church

What thoughts and feelings do you have about this place?

- What did it feel like when we were together listening, singing, and thinking about God?
- Look around you now – what does it feel like to be here? What do you like about this place?
- What do you think Christians like about coming to church?

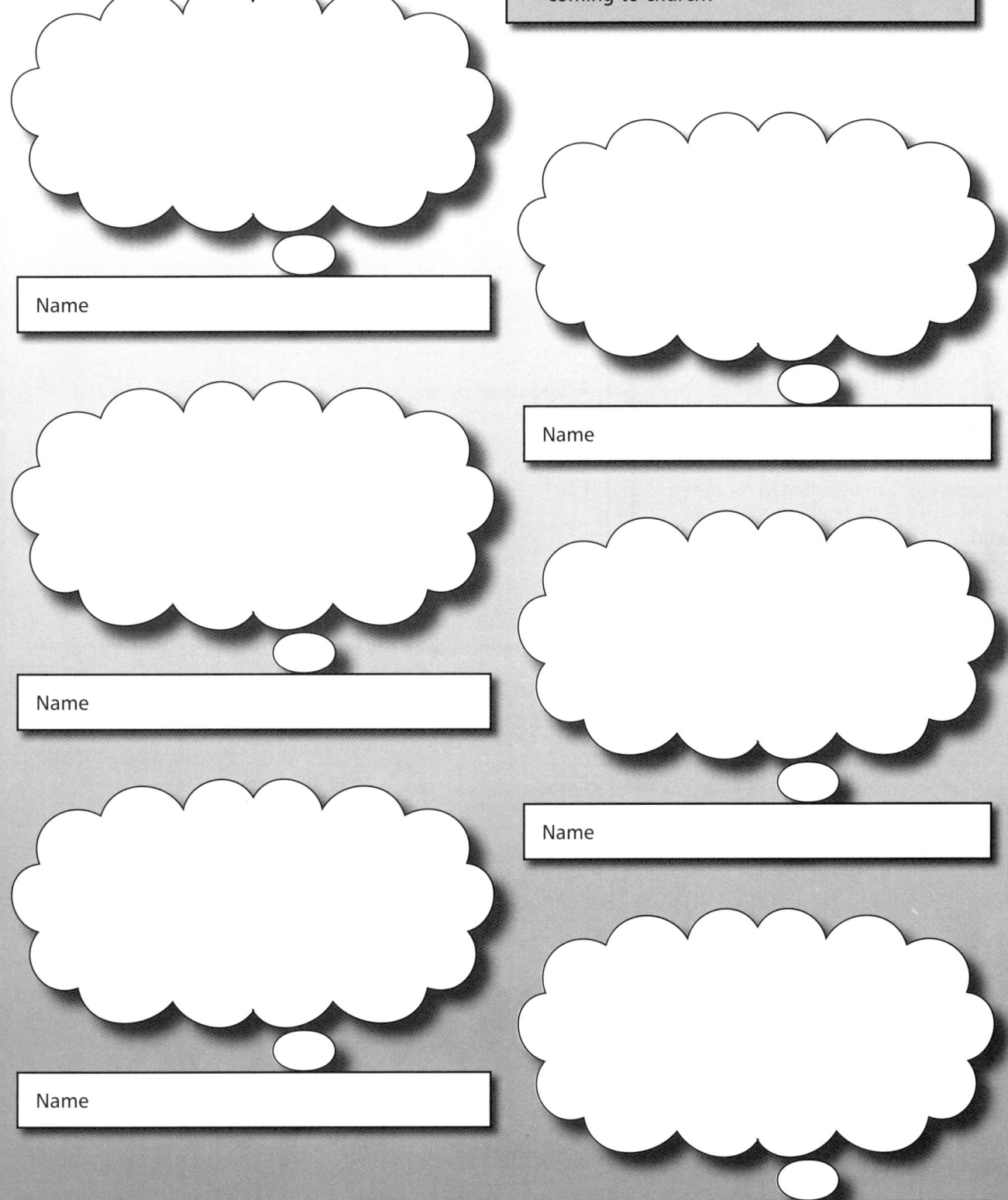

Name

Name

Name

Name

Name

Name

Name

© 2007 RE Today Services
Permission is granted to photocopy this page for use in classroom activities in schools that have purchased this publication.

What does it mean to belong to a Christian family at Christmas?

For the teacher

An appropriate way of exploring religion around you with younger pupils is to focus on the 'story' of a child or family who belongs to a particular religious tradition.

In this unit we focus on Sally and her Anglican (Church of England) Christian family at Christmas.

Two activities are suggested – each outlining a different 'way in' to help young children explore, and begin to understand, what Christmas means to a Christian family. The two strategies are

- Using story – Sally's Christmas
- Using an artefact – the Advent Ring.

These activities can be adapted for other religions and can be built into schemes of work to enable children to begin to understand the importance and value of religion and belief for some children and their families.

I can...

The following pupil-friendly criteria could be used to assess children's responses to the activities. Level 1 describes what most 6-year-olds should be able to do; Level 2 describes what most 7-year-olds should be able to do.

Level 1

I can...

- name three things that a Christian family might do at Christmas
- talk about an Advent ring, where you would see one and how it might be used
- talk about belonging: whom do I belong to and how it makes me feel to know I belong.

Level 2

I can...

- use religious words to tell the story of Sally and her Christian family at Christmas
- say why Sally lights a special candle leading up to Christmas
- talk about thoughts and feelings I have when I am celebrating a special day and say why this day is special.

Christian family at Christmas

5-7

For the teacher

As a starting point for learning about 'belonging to a Christian family', it is important for children to have the opportunity to reflect on their own experiences of belonging. Try the following game.

Where do I belong?

- Make a list of who/what the children belong to. This could include family, class, school, after-school club. It might include Rainbows or Beaver Scouts/ a group connected to a faith or an interest, perhaps a ballet or karate class, for example.

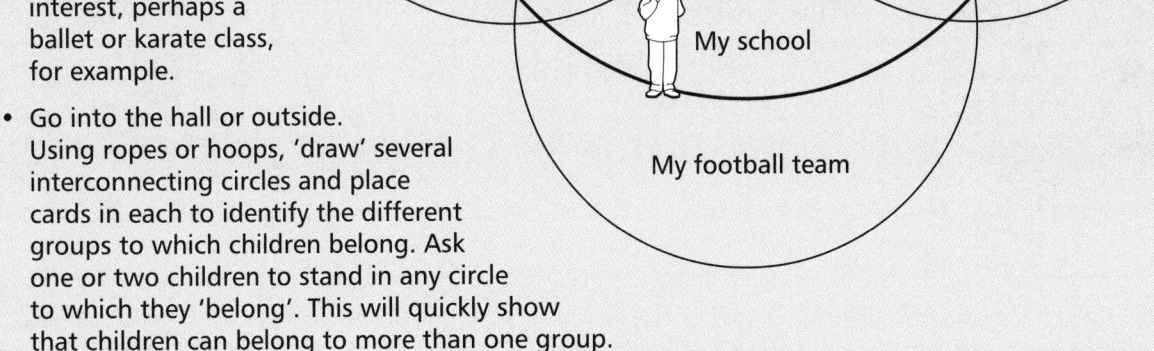

- Go into the hall or outside. Using ropes or hoops, 'draw' several interconnecting circles and place cards in each to identify the different groups to which children belong. Ask one or two children to stand in any circle to which they 'belong'. This will quickly show that children can belong to more than one group.

- Ask the children to bring to school a photo or something that shows they belong such as a badge or certificate. Use digital cameras to take photos of any groups children belong to in school, for example their class, friendship group or sports team. Children choose one photograph or object. Ask them to add a sentence to say how 'belonging' to that group makes them feel.

Where does Sally belong?

- Photocopy the cards on page 10 (downloadable for RE Today subscribers at www.retoday.org.uk). Make enough sets of cards for pairs of children to have a set each. Use these cards to introduce children to Sally. She is nearly 6 years old and has two older brothers and a younger sister. Sally and her family are Christians.

- The sentences from Sally on the next page describe what she does in her Christian family at Christmas.

Ask the children to

- sort the cards into activities that they might do in their family and those that they do not.
- sequence the cards to tell Sally's story.
- pick out one thing Sally does on Christmas Day which they think is very important to her as a Christian. Draw a picture to show this and write three sentences about why they picked this.

9

What does Sally do at Christmas?

I make Christmas cards.	I put up lots of decorations.	I light an Advent candle at home and at Church.
I have a crib at home and in Church.	We act out the story of Jesus being born in a stable to everyone in the church. I want to be an angel!	I give presents.
I sing Christmas carols.	I go to church on Christmas morning.	I read about Jesus in my Bible.
We have a special dinner on Christmas day.	I wake up early Christmas morning – I'm so excited.	I go to a Christmas party with my friends at Church.

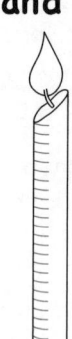

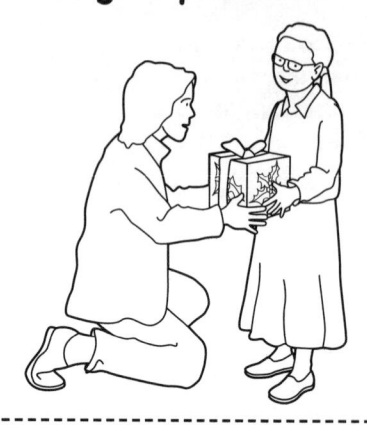

Christian family at Christmas

What is important to Sally and her family?

For the teacher

The following activities make use of the pictures on page 12. These can be photocopied or downloaded from the website.

- Give each group of pupils a copy of the pictures. Use Activity 1 to encourage children to look very carefully at the pictures to see what they can discover about Sally and her family.
- Share and talk about children's ideas with the whole class.
- Use the artefact activity (page 13) to explore the story behind Christmas and its meaning for Sally and her family.

Activity 1   Look and tell

This activity asks the children to reflect on religious and spiritual feelings and experiences.

Ask children to look carefully at the pictures.

With a partner talk about:

- What is Sally doing?
- How do you think Sally is feeling?
- Is she enjoying herself as she celebrates Christmas with her family and friends?
- Do you think Sally has any other feelings as she celebrates?

5-7

Activity 2   Pair and share

In pairs, children

- talk about a special day or time that they have celebrated. Did it involve any of the things that Sally is doing? (Singing? Lighting a special candle? Eating a special meal? Remembering a special story? Giving presents?)
- feedback their ideas to the rest of the group.

Explain to children that Christmas is very special for Christians like Sally because it celebrates the birth of Jesus. Christians, like Sally and her family, follow Jesus and try to be like him. They believe Jesus to be God's son.

- Ask children to pick out any special things Sally does which help her remember Jesus at Christmas.
- They could record their ideas in a 'Think Book'.

Activity 3   Creative activity

Children could create a Christmas card that Sally could give to some people living near her church, who might be feeling a little sad and lonely. The card should

- celebrate Christmas and invite them to a service at the church.
- show them what kind of things might be happening at church at Christmas.
- make the people want to come and join in.

Meeting Sally and her Christian family

This is the story of Sally.

The pictures show some activities that are really important to Sally.

Look carefully at your pictures. What do they tell you about Sally and her family?

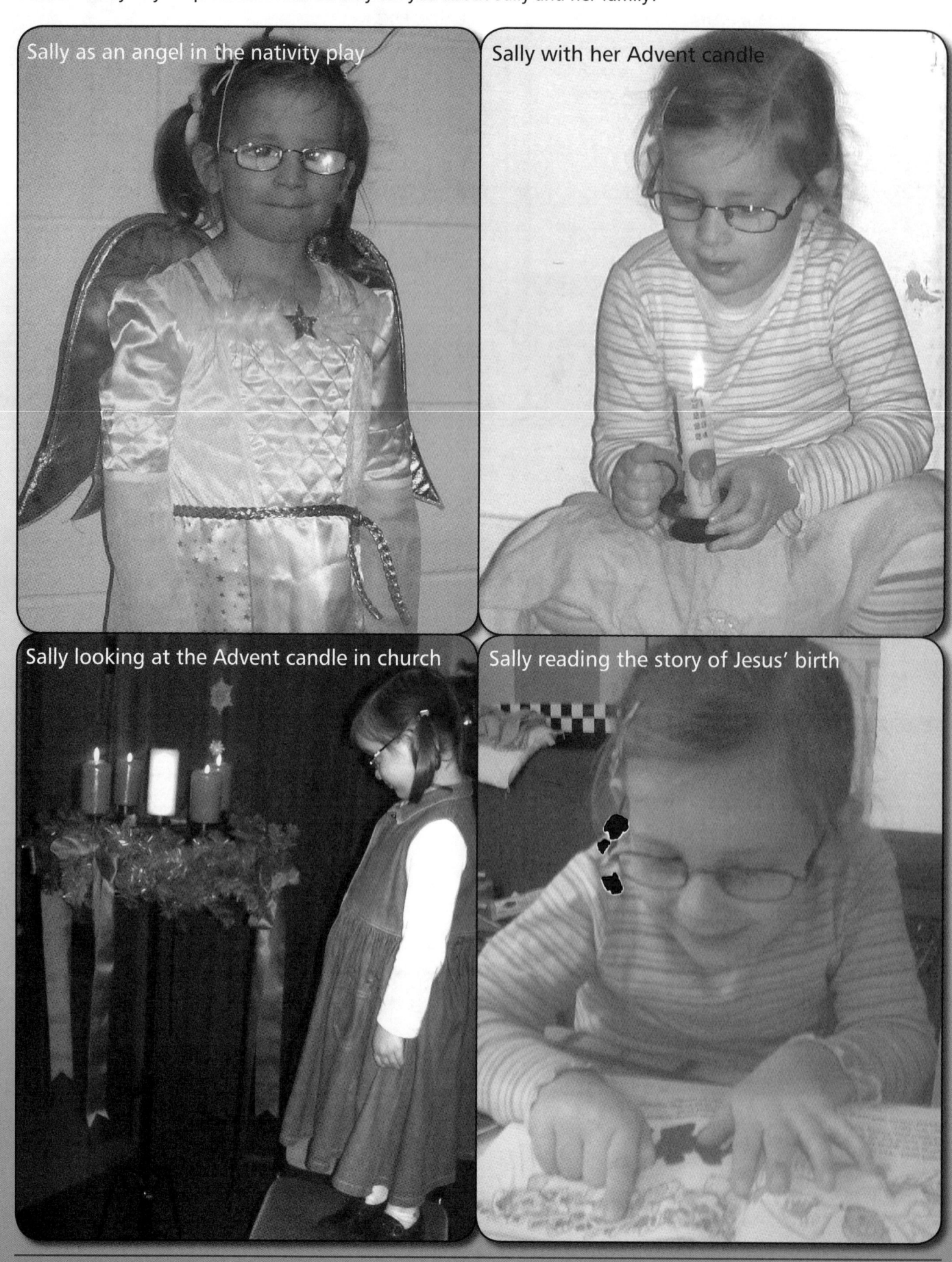

Sally as an angel in the nativity play

Sally with her Advent candle

Sally looking at the Advent candle in church

Sally reading the story of Jesus' birth

Christian family at Christmas

Engagement through the use of an artefact: an Advent ring

5-7

For the teacher

One of the artefacts that Sally has in her home and her church is an Advent candle. The following activity introduces the children to this artefact and its meaning for Christians.

Using an artefact

Use a feely box or bag and place within it an Advent ring (without any prickly plants attached) as used in a church.

Children could pass this around, feel it, and try to work out what might be inside.

Once the Advent ring is revealed, ask the children to respond to the following questions:

- What do you think it is?
- What do you think it might be used for?
- Where might it be used?
- Who would use this?
- Why do you think Sally has an Advent candle at home?

Explain to children that Sally uses her candle at home during Advent as she prepares for Christmas – a very special time celebrating the birthday of Jesus. It is a reminder each day that this very special time is coming.

For the teacher

Sally makes a link between the use of an Advent ring/wreath in church to the Advent candle she has at home. Sally is very excited with the countdown to Christmas Day and every morning she takes it in turns with her brothers and sister to light the candle and also to open the next door on the Advent calendar. Sally and her family will always say a short prayer when they light the candle, just as the vicar will say a prayer when he lights the Advent candles each Sunday in church during the season of Advent.

Pupil activity

- Listen as you hear the prayer that Sally and the rest of her family say together each morning when they light the candle.

  'We light this candle to welcome you,
  We light this candle to remember you,
  Thank you for the light you bring.'

- As the Advent candle is lit, sit quietly for a minute and think about who Sally is welcoming and remembering. Think about what Sally might like to say thank you for at Christmas. Why does she want to say thank you? What sorts of things would you like to say thank you for?

- Write a short thank-you prayer or reflection to say thank you for all the good things about belonging to your family or class or school.

Information on the symbolism of the Advent wreath can be found on the RE Today website: **www.retoday.org.uk**

Religion around us: a visual learning activity

For the teacher

If you were to ask children to give you some examples of religion around them, what would you expect them to say? The local church? The vicar? Christmas or Easter? If your school is located in a multi-cultural community, they may mention other non-Christian religions as well. Some children might even connect religion to bad things such as war and terrorism.

The activities in this section aim to deepen and broaden children's understanding of religion and how it is expressed. The line drawing on pages 16–17 provides a visual stimulus to engage children in thinking about the rich variety that religion might mean. It includes the easily observable aspects such as special buildings and symbols and introducing a range of values and activities which come under the heading of 'beliefs in action'. Even these represent only a fraction of the forms that religious commitment might take.

The following activities suggest some practical ways you might use the line drawing to get children thinking, speaking, reflecting and responding. You will think of others.

I can...

The following pupil-friendly criteria could be used to assess children's responses to the activities. Level 4 describes what most 11-year-olds should be able to do.

Level 3
- use a developing religious vocabulary to describe some key features of religion (AT1)
- *ask thoughtful questions about religion and belief (AT2).*

Level 4
- use a developing religious vocabulary to describe and show understanding of key features of religion (AT1)
- *raise and suggest answers to questions and issues raised by religion and belief (AT2).*

The line drawing and additional materials can be downloaded from the RE Today website for use by subscribers. Go to www.retoday.org.uk

1 Looking for religion around us
Activity

- From the picture list 10 items you think are connected with religion. Compare your list with a partner and tick any you have both chosen. Talk about the others you have included and explain why you picked them.
- Underline:
  - in red any that are buildings where religious groups meet;
  - in blue any that are to do with people helping others;
  - in black any that are to do with worship or special events in people's lives.
- Use your ideas to complete a paragraph starting with: 'I think religion is...'.

2 Take a tour
Activity

Imagine you work for the Tourist Board. A group of Japanese visitors want to know more about religion in Britain today. You are asked to plan a walking route around the town to show the tourists as many different aspects of religion as you can.

Look carefully at the picture. Think about:

- Where would you take them and why?
- Whom might they like to meet?
- What might they ask you?

Plan your route. Add any notes to your plan to help you answer any questions the tourists might ask you.

Religion around us

3 Be a reporter — Activity

Imagine you work at the local newspaper. Your editor wants a special feature about religion in your local community. He has asked you to write it!

Look carefully at the picture. Make some notes in preparation about:

- Whom you would interview and why.
- What questions you would ask.
- What photographs you would include.

Tip: religion is about what people believe, how and whom they worship, and how they live their everyday lives. Have you covered all these?

4 A community like mine? — Activity

Not all towns and villages are like the one shown in the drawing.

What does your town or community have that

- is similar to this one?
- is different from this one?

If you belong to a community with people of different religions, beliefs and customs – what are the best things about it?

If your community is very different to that in the picture, what do you think you would like best and least about living in the town in the picture?

7-11

5 Meet the people — Activity

- Look carefully at all the people in the picture - count them, guess their ages, suggest names for them.

- In a group of five, choose five people in the picture who you think would have something interesting to say about what they believe and how they live.

- If you could ask them to write about themselves for the town magazine, what do you think they would say? (You might need to find out more about some of them – how can you do this?)

- In your group, each member takes one character from the picture and writes 'their' paragraph. Put the paragraphs together into an article. Make into a booklet and design an appropriate front cover.

6 Where can we find 'religion'? — Activity

To understand what religion is and why it plays such an important part in many people's lives we need to look at:

1. A religion's teaching
2. The way religion helps people live their lives
3. The stories of a religion
4. The times when followers come together for worship
5. What a religion teaches about how its followers ought to behave
6. The ceremonies, rituals and celebrations of a religion.

In a group of three or six look at the picture – can you find any evidence for each of the above?

Make a poster to show your findings. Each member illustrates one or two of the above using his/her own ideas or those taken from the picture. It could show the six aspects linked together. Add your own thoughts in speech bubbles. Decide on an appropriate title.

© 2007 RE Today Services
Permission is granted to photocopy this page for use in classroom activities in schools that have purchased this publication.

SAVE THE PLANET

SAVE THE PLANET

SAVE THE EARTH

BOOKSHOP

NEWSAGENT

TOM'S FRUIT & VEG

YOGA
7PM
TUE

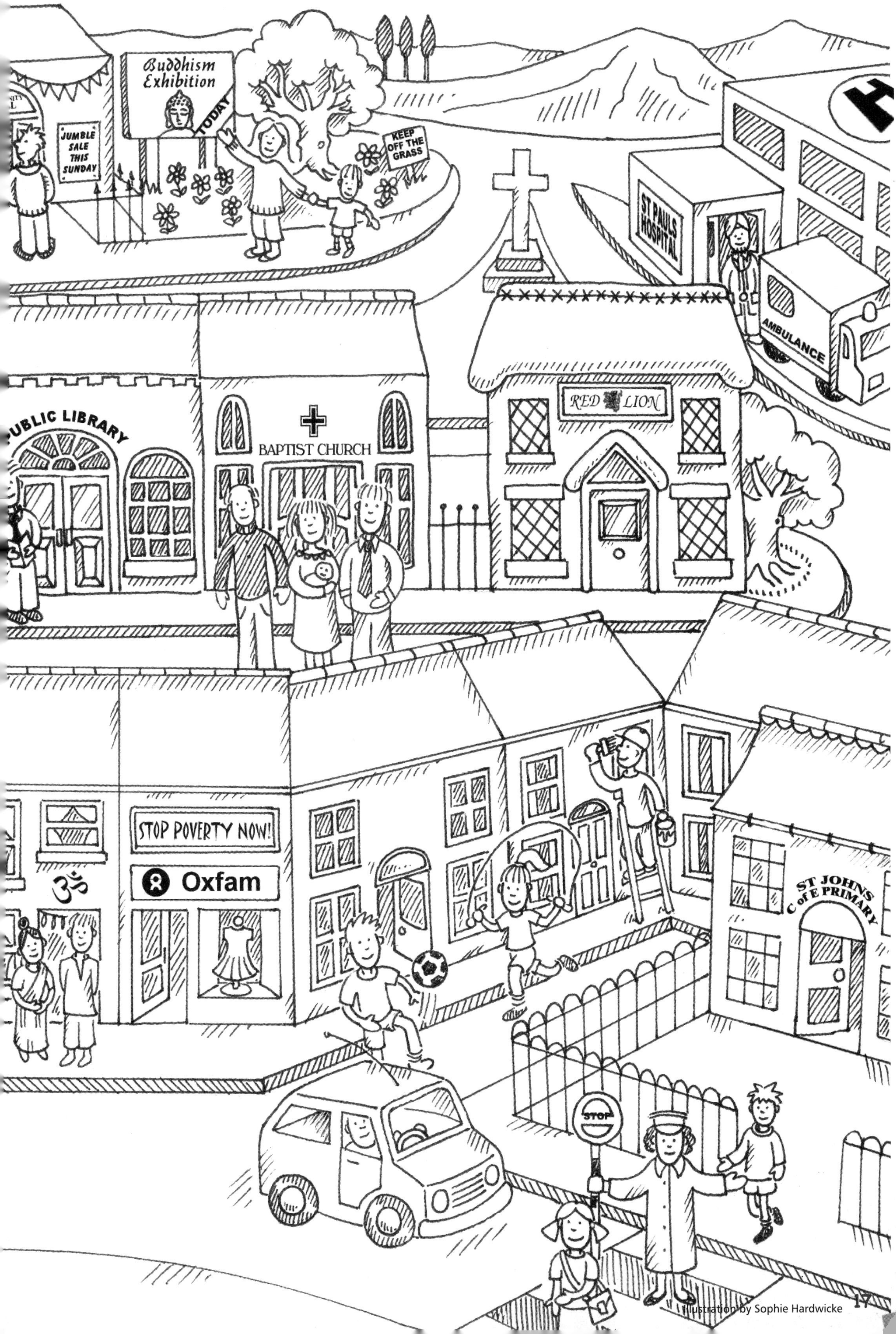

Illustration by Sophie Hardwicke

Meet Nathan

Nathan is 8 and lives with his parents and brother in Hereford. The family are Roman Catholic Christians.

What's the best thing for you about being a Catholic?

The best thing for me is going to Church every Sunday with my family. I like the singing, listening during the mass and meeting all my friends. I am an altar server – I really enjoy that. At the beginning of mass I sometimes go out to another room for the Children's Liturgy – I often carry the banner or the Bible. I always answer the questions when we talk about the Gospel story.

Another good thing about being a Catholic is saying my prayers. Before I say any prayers, I always make the sign of the cross, saying 'In the name of the Father, the Son and the Holy Spirit, Amen'. I say my prayers every night. I also say the 'Hail Mary'. I ask Mary (Jesus' mother) to pray for me too. I asked God to make my Mum better when she was ill this year. We say 'Grace' before we have our family Sunday lunch. I go to a Catholic school and we say prayers there too and sometimes have a mass.

What is the most special day in your religion?

Christmas is great. We get ready for Christmas in our family by reading the Bible together after tea on a Sunday. We have a wooden crib in our sitting room and before Christmas the Priest comes to our house and blesses it.

I had a very exciting day last year – I made my First Communion. I dressed smartly with a new waistcoat, all my family came to the mass, and I received Jesus in the host (special bread) and wine for the first time. Before that, Father Nicholas had just given me a blessing. I felt very grown-up and special. Afterwards we had a big party with a bouncy castle, and I had lots of lovely presents.

What would change about your religion?

I really can't think of anything I would change – I just like all of it.

What is your favourite story from your religion?

There are lots of stories I like – my Bible story book is one of my favourite books to read. It was given to me when I was baptised. I like the stories and the pictures. Two of my favourite stories are when Peter catches many fish and when Jesus heals the man lowered through the roof by his friends.

Imagine you could ask God a question, what would it be?

'Why can't every day be a sunny day?' I love playing outside – I'm very good at swingball, tennis and cricket, so I'd like it to be sunny every day.

Meet Nathan

Classroom activities

Exploring a favourite story about Jesus
Activity

- Read or tell the story of Jesus healing the man lowered through the roof (Mark ch.2, vs 1-12).
- Children act out the story. Groups show their role-play, freeze-framing important points in the story. Teacher taps the shoulder of various characters who then share the thoughts and feelings of their character 'in role'. What questions would the children like to ask the characters involved?
- Record 'freeze-frames' with a digital camera. Using speech bubbles, children record thoughts and feelings of characters in the story and add to the images. What do you think this story tells us about Jesus that is important to Nathan?

Exploring making the sign of the cross
Activity

- Show a video clip of someone making the sign of the cross, or demonstrate – trace out a large cross from forehead to chest and from shoulder to shoulder with the right hand.
- When have children seen someone making the sign of the cross? Perhaps before someone prays, or as they enter a church; a priest or minister blessing a person or congregation; a Roman Catholic (or Eastern Orthodox) sports competitor before the start of a race or match.
- Ask the children why they think a Roman Catholic Christian might make the sign of the cross and say 'In the name of the Father, Son and Holy Spirit, Amen.' It is a reminder of Jesus dying on a cross and rising again; a time when the person focuses on God; a dedication of what is to come to God as Father, Son and Holy Spirit; an outward sign of belief.
- Ask children to think about what they believe in that they are prepared to stand up and declare. Think, pair, share a value, belief or code they feel is important enough to tell everyone.
- In a Reflection circle, pupils take it in turns to share their thoughts with the starter 'I believe...'.

Exploring First Holy Communion
Activity

7-11

- Watch BBC video 'Pathways of Belief – Christianity' which shows a child receiving First Communion. (See also RE Quest CD-ROM or website www.request.org.uk/ section on Communion.)
- In groups, pupils anonymously write out on slips of paper any questions they would like to ask about the communion service. Put the questions into a question box, redistribute the slips of paper and ask pupils to attempt to answer the questions in their groups. Discuss main themes as a class. Talk about why First Communion was such a special day for Nathan and for the child in the video.
- Invite a Catholic priest (or practising Roman Catholic lay person) to meet the class and answer children's questions. Ask him if it would be possible to bring unconsecrated wafers for the children to see. Send him the questions in advance and brief him on the ability and interests of the children.
- As a follow-up, pupils could send the priest a thank-you letter, identifying what they found most interesting about the visit and what they had learned.

I can...
By the end of this unit, pupils working at level 3 (most 9-year-olds) should be able to:

- suggest why Roman Catholics make the sign of the cross and think of a belief or value that is important in their own life
- suggest the meaning of a service of Holy Communion; raise and suggest answers to questions about Roman Catholic beliefs about Holy Communion.

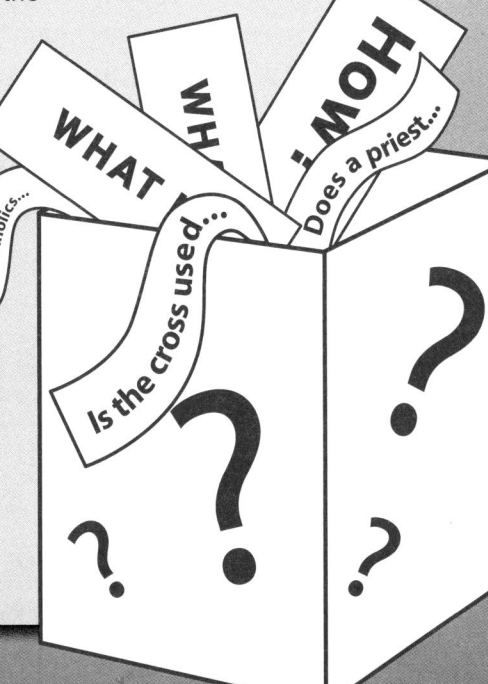

Meet Dora

Dora is 11 and lives with her parents in Bournville, Birmingham. Dora has been a Quaker all her life; her mum and dad are Quakers too.

What's the best thing for you about being a Quaker?

The best thing about Quakers is that everyone is treated equally. The children are treated like adults and they can be given responsibilities. Children take part in the services; they can do all the things grown-ups can do. Men and women are the same too.

Quakers believe in God. I think God is an 'it' not a 'he' or 'she'. God is with us all the time. Quakers believe we all have an equal part in God. Jesus settled things and made them right. Quakers talk about things in their own way and understand that we are each different.

I have sometimes taken part in peace vigils. There was one on the main road going into Birmingham. We held banners like 'Not in my name. Don't attack Iraq'. Basically it was a protest against war.

At our meeting children come in for the first ten minutes and then we go out and do other stuff. One term we did Bible stories, sometimes we do about Quaker testimonies or make things.

The grown-ups meet for an hour. There is no one in charge. People can minister if they want. They can say about things they think they need to say, if they feel they really should in their hearts. Some people just read books like *Advices and Queries* and *Quaker Faith and Practice*, and sometimes the Bible.

We have people sometimes who say things from *Quaker Faith and Practice*. It is a book with lots of different quotes from Quakers through history and people read out things that strike them as important for the day.

What is the most special day in your religion?

The time I like best is **Yearly Meeting**. It is a gathering of Quakers from all over the country. It is good to meet people you haven't met before. You don't have to be specially chosen to go.

What is your favourite story from your religion?

My favourite story is **'The Children of Reading Meeting'**. It is the true story of when the adults got taken to prison because the government was scared of religious sects, but the children kept the Quaker meeting going while the adults were locked away. It shows everyone being equal and taking responsibilities.

(The story is told on this website: www.westhillsfriends.org/QVWchildren.html.)

Imagine you could ask God some questions, what would they be?

I would like to ask God:

- How can we make world peace?
- How can we make the world a better place for everyone in it and so that everyone would be happy?

Meet Dora

Classroom activities

For the teacher

In this interview Dora talks clearly and powerfully about things she feels strongly about and why, and that she is willing to take action. This provides excellent stimulus to upper primary pupils not only to demonstrate their understanding of Dora's beliefs, but also to reflect on the extent to which their own beliefs and values impact on their actions.

The following pupil-friendly criteria could be used to assess pupil's responses to this activity.

I can...

Level 3

- **make a link** between Dora's belief in God and how she lives her life
- *describe* the ways in which some Christians react to unfairness, making a link to what matters to me.

Level 4

- **show that I understand** why Dora's Christian beliefs are important to her and can describe how they impact on her life.

Activity 1 Thinking about local news

- Pupils work in pairs to **read** Dora's interview. They **highlight** key words which show the links between what Dora believes and what she does.
- As a class (or in groups) pupils **log on** to 'BBC Local News – Where I live' (www.bbc.co.uk/whereilive) and **identify** two or three local stories about issues which they think Dora would be interested in. Ask children to **talk about**:
  - Why do they think Dora would be interested in the chosen story/stories?
  - What sort of action might Dora take / not take?
  - What is the pupils' own reaction to these stories? What, if anything, might they take action about? What sort of action?

Activity 2 Creating a multimedia presentation

- Working in groups, pupils **choose** one of the news items from Activity 1 and **create a multimedia presentation** about the issue from Dora's point of view, suitable to be sent to the editor of the BBC Local News website.
- **Useful resources include:** the quotations on the right; www.quaker.org.uk; http://en.wikipedia.org/wiki/Quaker.

> Happy are the peacemakers, for they shall be called the children of God.
> *Christian Bible, Matthew ch.5, v.9*

> People matter. In the end human rights are about people being treated and feeling like people who matter.
> *Quaker Faith and Practice, 24:29*

> Respect the laws of the state but let your first loyalty be to God's purposes. If you feel impelled by strong conviction to break the law, search your conscience deeply.
> *Quaker Advices and Queries, 35*

> I think it is very important for people to help each other out. I actually ran a fundraising event for a school in South Africa. I did that because on a family holiday I saw the poverty that had ruined the otherwise beautiful country and I couldn't leave without vowing to make some sort of difference
> *Christian, female, aged 13*

7-11

Meet Alice

Alice is 11 and goes to the Dharma School, Brighton. It's the only Buddhist primary school in Britain. Children of other faiths, as well as Buddhists, attend the school.

What do you like about being a Buddhist?

The best thing for me is that I like **meditating**. It's special to me because it's the only quiet time in the day.

What is the most special day in your religion?

The most special day in the year for me is **Wesak**. I like Wesak because when my school celebrated the festival we did some fun stuff. We painted a big **mandala** in the playground and we wrote some of our own wishes on **bodhi** leaves (they come from a kind of fig tree). We hung them on a tree. Wesak is the day we remember the **birth of the Buddha** (so it's a kind of birthday celebration), and his enlightenment, and his death! Wesak is on the full moon day, in May.

What is your favourite story from your religion?

My favourite Buddhist story is one about a hurt swan. I like it because it's an interesting story, and our version has some great illustrations. This story happened when Siddhartha was 7. He was out in the woods with his cousin Devadatta. They saw a swan. Quickly, Devadatta shot the swan with an arrow. Siddhartha rushed to the wounded swan and pulled out the arrow. He took the bird gently in his arms. Devadatta shouted 'Give me the swan. I shot it. It's mine!'

'I'll never give it to you: you'll kill it!' said the prince. 'Let's ask the ministers of the court to decide whose it is.'

They had different views. Some said, 'The swan should be given to Devadatta.' Others said, 'It should go to Prince Siddhartha.' At last, one wise minister stood up and said: 'A life belongs to one who saves it, not to one who will destroy it. The swan goes to the prince.' Siddhartha took care of the swan until it could fly again. Then he set the bird free.

Would you like to ask the Buddha some questions? How do you think he would answer?

I'd like to be able to ask the Buddha some questions. I would ask him:

- Why is there so much suffering?
- Why is there war?
- What made you want to be the Buddha?

Here are the answers I think he would give:
There is lots of suffering because everything changes. War happens because people fight over land, or they might even think it's fun to fight. I wanted to become the Buddha because I wanted to help people.

Meet Alice

Activities with Alice's interview

1 Similar and different

Begin by asking pupils to make a list of things that sometimes happen on a birthday. Then get them to find out more about Wesak, the day Alice likes best. At Wesak, celebrations vary, but include:

- Carrying lanterns in processions
- Meditating and chanting
- Giving generously to monks and nuns
- Sharing food at the Vihara
- Setting up a 'free food' stall on the streets
- Keeping extra religious rules
- Remembering the life and death of the Buddha.

A writing task: Ask pupils to make a 'seven senses' grid that shows: what do you see/touch/taste/smell/hear/feel/think at a birthday celebration? Then make another: what might a Buddhist like Alice see/touch/taste/smell/hear/feel/think at Wesak?

2 The biggest questions

Alice's questions to the Buddha are not easy. They matter because they are some of life's biggest questions. Ask the pupils to write down some of their own biggest questions. Discuss with them where we go for answers to these puzzling mysteries. Pupils might devise an interview with the wisest person on earth, or with God: they write down a few of the biggest questions they can think of, then shuffle them all up. In pairs, they then work out what they think the Wise, Divine or Enlightened might say in answering the questions.

Additional work: There is an 'interview with the Buddha' created by Alice's class at the Dharma School on the RE Today subscribers' website. Download it, and use it with your class.

3 Going to a religious school

Alice goes to a Buddhist school. Lots of children in the UK go to religious schools, including many who are not from religious families. We asked Alice's classmates about this. Here are some of the things they liked:

'We learn a lot about meditation: it's special because we sit down and calm down, and think about our thoughts.' *Scarlett*

'At Wesak you can make a liquid from the four elements. We drop wax (**earth**) from a candle (**fire**) through the **air** into a bowl of water. Then we spray it around!' *Ben*

'We find it OK to be silent.' *Lauren*

'I've learned to respect everything and everyone, and not to harm any living creature.' *Robin*

Talk about whether religious schools might be better at teaching these kinds of lessons – or can they be learned at any school?

4 Flash book: Rahula

An excellent flash book to show on your whiteboard, or pupils can use it on a computer workstation.

http://www.buddhanet.net/flash/rahula/rahula.html

This is the website of the Buddha Dharma Education Association. The story this flash book tells has interesting connections with the story of 'Siddhartha and the Swan' that Alice really likes. Ask pupils to read the flash book together, and then to think about and discuss how the two stories are connected. They should try to write about at least three connections between the story of the swan and the story of Rahula. In a class plenary, or circle time, ask children to say what they learned from the two stories for themselves. Ask them to give an example of when someone's kindness to animals impressed them.

7-11

A recommended resource

Adiccabandhu and Padmasri, *Siddhartha and the Swan*, Windhorse Publications 1998,

ISBN: 978-1-899579-10-5, 32 pages, paperback.

Meet Rohit

Rohit is 10 and lives with his family in Coventry. He and his family are Hindu.

What's the best thing about being a Hindu?

I think that the best thing about being a Hindu is having so many different festivals to celebrate. I enjoy celebrating the festivals of Holi, Navaratri, Diwali and Lord Krishna's birthday.

What is the most special day in your religion?

The most special time is **Navaratri**, because we get to go to the temple for nine days and we get to pray.

Nine days is a long time, isn't it? What else do you do?

We listen to the songs. We also have to do dances and competitions – the competition is to see who looks the best and you have special clothes for it. We get the clothes from India; we go and get them ourselves. We have new clothes every year and my family all go in the summer holidays. We get them from Bombay, for me and my brother. My mum has saris. I have won 5 times. I got this real gold thing of a god's statue. Real gold.

Is Lord Krishna the god that you and your family feel is a special god?

We think they're all special. Lord Krishna is the most important. When someone is in trouble he does spirit things and he goes to the house and helps.

In your house do you have a special murti for you and your family?

We have **Ganesh, Krishna** and **Gayatri**. Krishna comes to the house to help; if one person needs help only that one person can see him. My brother was once doing a quiz in school and he needed help, so he called on Krishna.

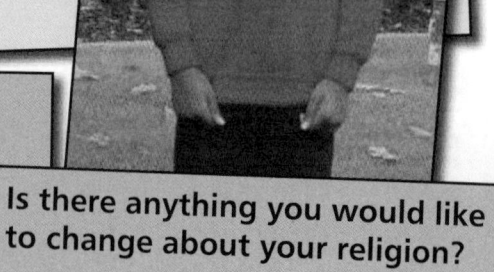

Is there anything you would like to change about your religion?

No, I wouldn't want to change anything about my religion; it's all fine as it is.

What is your favourite story from your religion?

My favourite story is the **Diwali** story.

Why is this your favourite story?

Because in this story it says how good people defeat evil people.

Imagine that you could ask God three questions. What would they be?

The three questions I would ask are:

- Why did you make the world?
- How did you make the religion?
- How many Hindu Gods are there?

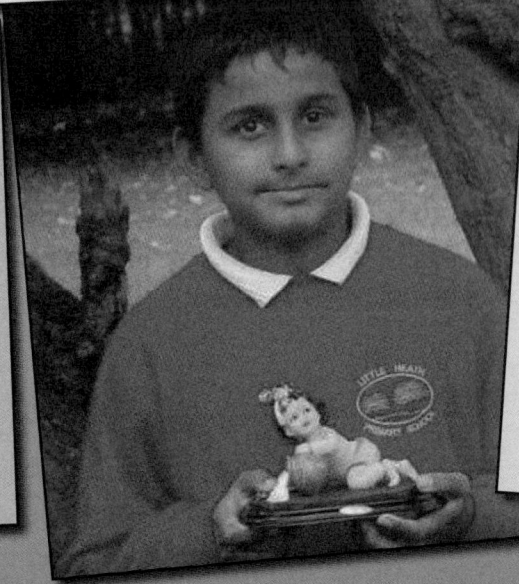

Meet Rohit

For the teacher

The activities suggested here focus on Rohit's favourite activity of worship in the temple (mandir).

- Show children pictures of a Hindu shrine or go on a virtual tour of a Hindu temple. The centrepiece of both a temple and shrine will be an image of one of the Hindu Gods.

- Use a picture or **murti** of Lord Krishna. Pupils could create a shrine for the classroom adding objects used in worship in a temple. Can the pupils think of two objects to feel, two to smell, two to listen to, two tastes they may experience and two that are particularly pleasing to see. Use all five senses for their shrine. Think about which senses are used by Hindus in worship to show their devotion to the gods and goddesses.

- Set up a shrine in the classroom before the pupils enter the room. Keep it hidden behind a curtain. In groups of four, pupils spend a few moments looking at it before working together to recreate a picture of what they saw. Keep the shrine covered until they have completed their task. Open it to view. Ask pupils to compare their own with 'the hidden shrine' and identify what they see and suggest how and why the shrine is used by worshippers.

- Talk with a partner about what makes a place special. What makes a place of worship, such as a mandir, special and sacred? Say why they think Rohit likes to go to the temple to pray, what makes this a special place and time for him?

  Describe something – a time, a place, an activity – which they find spiritual or inspiring. Share it with a partner. Use art, colour or writing to express it.

- Pupils could create an information leaflet for visitors to the temple, describing some of the features of Hindu worship, including the use of songs and prayers.

Information file Navaratri

- The word Navaratri actually means nine (Nava) nights (ratri).
- Navaratri is the worship of the three divine goddesses:
- **Saraswati** Goddess of learning and speech
- **Lakshmi** Goddess of wealth and prosperity
- **Durga** Goddess of strength and courage.
- There are grand processions of all gods and goddesses on the third day of the festival signifying the victory of the good over the wicked.
- The most significant part of the festival is the setting up of steps, always an odd number, and then the placing of the **murtis** on them.

7–11

I can...

The following pupil-friendly criteria could be used to assess children's responses to the activities. Level 3 describes what most 8–9 year olds should be able to do. **I can...**

Level 3

- Use some religious words to describe a Hindu shrine
- Ask some good questions about why a Hindu would choose to attend a mandir.

Level 4

- Describe four ways in which Hindu worship shows devotion to the Gods and Goddesses
- Suggest some reasons why a particular god or goddess is special or inspirational for a Hindu.

See also

www.reonline.org.uk/allre/tt_links.php?139

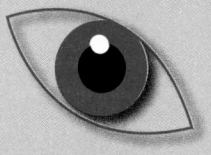

Virtual tour of Hindu mandir.

www.btinternet.com/~vivekananda/schools.htm

This is a good, large general Hindu site and there is a virtual puja to try.

Meet Yahya

Yahya is 10 and lives with his parents, his brother and two sisters in Gloucester. They are Muslims, following the religion of Islam.

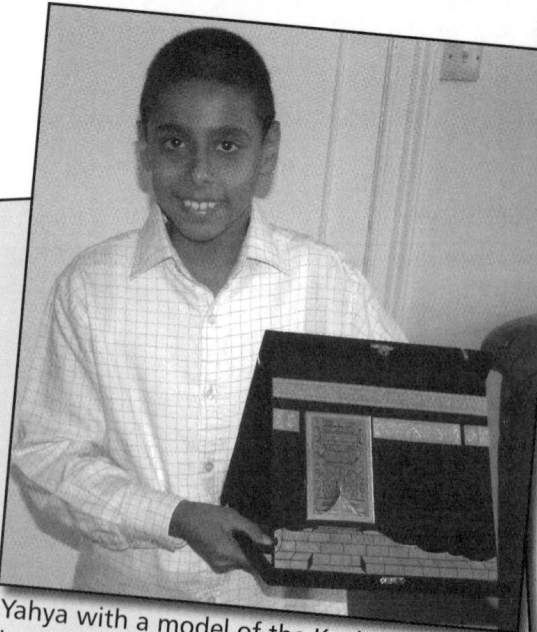

Yahya with a model of the Kaaba he visited in Makkah.

What's the best thing for you about being a Muslim?

The thing I like best is being part of a community, helping each other, being peaceful together, worshipping **Allah**. I meet with others at the madrassah to learn to read the **Qur'an** and to learn about what's right and wrong.

I go to the **mosque** when I can. I can't go to all the prayers, some are early morning when I am sleeping, others late at night. I try to go to one during the day, especially during **Ramadan**. If you miss one you are able to read the prayer afterwards. At school I try to do the prayer at lunchtime. This year (Year 6), I have done it on my own. Last year, when I was Year 5, there were others with me. I like to do the prayer – I even tell my granddad that it's time for prayer.

On Fridays we have a special prayer but on school days I can't go, but in holidays I can. What I really like is that I'm treated like everyone else at the mosque – we are all equal. Our religion teaches us to treat each other with respect and all the same, whether they are old or young, rich and poor. Yes, I like going to the mosque.

What is the most special day in your religion?

The two Eids. **Eid ul Fitr** and **Eid ul Adha**. These are days of celebration, really enjoying yourself. You have fasted for the first Eid, so it is a fun day, lots of happiness after the **fast**. I enjoy fasting – it's like a test you set for yourself to show that you can do it. It's a time when you behave, because sometimes I can be naughty. For this month I have to have control over myself. Dad describes it as 'recharging your batteries'. Fasting helps you live properly for the rest of the year. If you have something hard to do, you know you can do it, because you have already done something hard.

What would you like to change about your religion?

I'd change the prayer times! I'd make them closer together so that you can get other things done. Dad says they are spread across the day to help me remember God in all I do.

What is your favourite story from your religion?

I've just been on holiday to Makkah. I'm reading a story I got when I was there about one of the Prophet's companions who He called 'The Nation's Trustworthy'. Our prophet had chosen this man to take some money to someone. I think it's good to be trustworthy like him.

What questions would you ask Allah if you could? (and what do you think might be the answers?)

I would ask Allah **'What pleases you most?'**

I think he might say praying to him, doing good deeds, giving to charity, making sure all your actions have sincere intentions – if you do something make sure you do it for the right reasons.

I would ask God 'Why did you create everything like it is?'

Meet Yahya

Activity | **7-11**

Classroom activity: What matters most to Yahya?

'Mysteries' is a thinking skills strategy which is very useful in the mixed age and ability classroom as it allows for various levels of response. It gets pupils talking about their learning and thinking processes.

- After reading the interview with Yahya, pupils are given a question to answer or a problem to solve, e.g. 'What matters most to Yahya?'
- They are then given clues, usually in the form of statement cards, which they have to sort through and make sense of, to agree on and produce a plausible answer. 'Red herrings' add fun and challenge.
- Explain to pupils that they are going to work like detectives to solve a question by looking through clues. Explain that it is the quality of thinking which matters, that there are not necessarily 'right' answers, just some more or less plausible ones.
- Ask pupils to feed back their answers to the class with a full explanation.
- It is useful to discuss how they did the activity so that they become aware of effective ways of working which they can apply again in future (e.g. What did you do with the cards first? Why?).
- Use the opportunity this activity provides to encourage pupils to reflect on their own values – what matters most to them? Talk about how these influence the things they do and the choices they make.

remembering God in all he does	playing football	going on holiday
having fun	worshipping Allah	being with his Granddad
reading the Q'ur'an	going to the Mosque	taking part in the Fast
doing good things for other people	being treated like an adult	belonging to a community
his family	being like everyone else	praying five times a day
doing well at school	being trustworthy	doing what's right

I can...

The following pupil-friendly criteria could be used to assess pupil's responses to this activity.

I can...

- sort relevant information from irrelevant and explain my ideas about what matters most to Yahya, a young Muslim. (L4 AT1)
- make links between what matters most to me and what matters most to Yahya, explaining my ideas thoughtfully. (L4 AT2)

See also

Another activity which links well to Yahya's interview uses Muslim children's quotes to explore the question 'Why is prayer so important to Muslims?' It can be found in *Symbols of Faith*, Developing Primary RE series, RE Today 2004 (ISBN 978-1-904024-47-7).

© 2006 RE Today Services
Permission is granted to photocopy this page for use in classroom activities in schools that have purchased this publication.

Meet Samuel

Samuel is 8. He lives with his parents and two sisters in the London Borough of Redbridge.

What's the best thing for you about being a Jew?

For me it's about being together with my family at special times. On Chanukah and Pesach we spend time together and I see people I haven't seen for a long time. Most special to me is my mum, dad and sisters, my cousins and of course my grandparents. I love festivals, especially Chanukah – you get presents, play dreidel, and light the menorah. Where we live they have a big menorah in the middle of the roundabout and I went to see it lit on the last night. I have my own menorah at home – shaped like a train – and I light it myself.

What is the most special day in your religion?

Shabbat – every Friday night, me and my sisters say the brocha for the candles. On Shabbat we have a rest. Most Shabbats I go to the children's service and we have our own kiddush. Boys open the Aron Hakodesh, and carry the Torah scrolls around. Another special time is Simchat Torah. Last year I was chatan bereshit. I was one of the oldest and had to help clearing up. I got a special certificate – I'm very proud of it.

What would you like to change about your religion?

I would change Yom Kippur so I can watch TV. We never watch TV on Yom Kippur because it's a serious day. I also worry about adults fasting. I worry they will get ill and not make it. I wish every festival was like Hanukkah.

What is your favourite story from your religion?

I like it when Moshe (Moses) came down from Ha'Sinai and smashed the tablets. It teaches us one of the Ten Commandments – not to worship idols. I think Moshe would be a kind person to meet, but also quite strict. If he saw things that weren't the Jewish way to behave he would get very angry.

Imagine that you could ask God three questions. What would they be?

Why are we alive? I think Hashem wants to give people their lives to learn to do things – like how to walk, talk and ride a bike and also how to help others. I go to Jewish Cubs and for my Home Help badge I helped my mum make a pizza.

Why do the festivals have those names?

What is my future? I would like to be a builder. I would also like a house with nice things inside and a car.

Meet Samuel

What would we do without festivals and special times?

For the teacher

Reading Samuel's interview, you might well be struck by the frequent and enthusiastic references to **festivals** and other **special times**! Clearly these are an important part of Samuel's religious and family life. His comments provide an excellent 'way in' to help pupils think deeply about the role of festivals and special times in their life too, whether or not they follow a particular faith tradition.

The following pupil-friendly criteria could be used to assess pupil's responses to this activity. Most 9-year-olds should be working at Level 3, most 11-year-olds at Level 4.

I can.....

Level 3

- **suggest** what difference festivals and special times make to Samuel's life
- **make meaningful links** between some Jewish festivals and special times, and my own.

Level 4

- **show my understanding** of the importance of festivals and special times for Samuel
- **respond meaningfully** to questions about festivals and special times in the light of my learning in RE.

Activity 1 Similarities and differences

- Pupils work in pairs/threes to **read** Samuel's interview. They **highlight** key words which show how Samuel feels about the festivals and special times he talks about. Two groups then join up to **share** ideas and to **agree** on five key words to share with the whole class.

- Working again in pairs/threes, pupils **identify** a religious or secular festival or special time which is important to them. They **talk about** the festival story, how the occasion is celebrated, and what it means to them. They then **map their ideas** onto a Venn diagram (see below). This will visually display areas of similarity and difference.

What do they notice about the things they share with Samuel? What about the differences? Does anything surprise them? Why/why not?

Thinking about festivals and special times

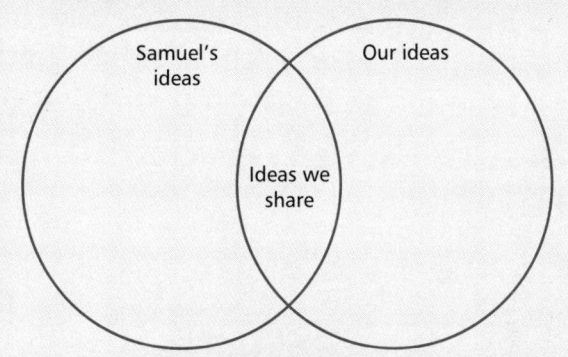

(Venn diagram: Samuel's ideas | Ideas we share | Our ideas)

See also

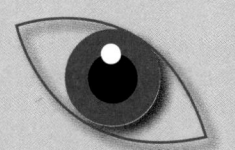

- **Glossary of terms**
  www.ritualwell.org/resources/glossary.

- **The Jewish Connection**
  A resource for young people focusing on life in one small Jewish congregation.
  www.spirit-staffs.co.uk/synagogue/index1.htm.

- **CLEO**
  Digital video resources for RE: 'Tefillin & tallit' and 'Morning prayers'
  www.cleo.net.uk/resources/index.php?ks=2&cur=15.

- **BBC Religion: Judaism**
  A vast resource on many aspects of Judaism
  www.bbc.co.uk/religion/religions/judaism/index.shtml.

Activity 2 What if there were no special times?

Drawing on their findings in Activity 1, pupils **talk** about and then **write** about:

- **How would Samuel feel** if all festivals and special times were cancelled, if they were no longer part of his life?
- **What difference would it make** to your family/school/town/country if there were no more festivals or special times?

7-11

Meet Eeshar

Eeshar is 8 and lives with his parents in Leeds. They are Sikhs.

What's the best thing for you about being a Sikh?

The best thing about being a Sikh is that I have 11 Beautiful Gurus who have taught Sikhs lots of nice things like **Seva** and **Simran**. When I do Seva (helping others) it makes me feel proud that I'm helping others and that means I'm helping the Guru. When I do Simran (Prayers/Meditation) it makes me feel calm and happy inside.

What would you like to change about your religion?

No, I think the Gurus have done a very good job and there is nothing that I would change. However, it would be nice to see more traditional Sikh instruments such as the santoor used in **gurdwaras** rather than the European harmonium.

What is the most special day in your religion?

Baisakhi is my favourite day because I can dress up in my Bana (Sikh uniform) which reminds me of **Guru Gobind Singh** Ji's younger sons, who were my age. Also I can take part in the **Nagar Kirtan**, which is a special procession through the streets near to where I live; once I was allowed to lead the procession which was really good.

What is your favourite story from your religion?

The Baisakhi story is my favourite story because it's amazing how the **Panj Pyare** came forward to give their lives to Guru Gobind Singh Ji, and it's amazing how Guru Gobind Singh Ji brought them back to life; only Guru Gobind Singh Ji could do such an amazing thing.

Imagine that you could ask God three questions. What would they be?

I would like to ask God to make it possible for me to see the 10 Gurus in human form. My dad says that we can meet the Gurus through the **Shabads** (Hymns) but I would love to actually see them.

I would also ask God to make it possible for me to be able to perform **Kirtan** in the **Golden Temple**. I think that would be really exciting, it would be brill.

I would also ask God to make the world a kinder place and stop all these bombings and killing people – we should all live together in peace.

Meet Eeshar

Activities

Exploring Eeshar's feelings

In pairs or individually pupils could:

- read the interview with Eeshar.
- identify Esher's feelings. (The chart below provides a summary of these for teacher reference.)
- Take each key feeling in turn and talk/write about a time when they have felt the same. For example: 'A time I felt proud was....'. 'Something which makes me feel excited is...'.

Responding to questions

- Children could respond to the five questions (these can be adapted for non-faith or non-practising children: examples are available for subscribers on the RE Today website).
- Compare personal answers with Eeshar's, looking for similarities and differences. Complete the following, in no more than 50 words: 'Eeshar's words have made me think about...'

Activity

Information file

Eeshar speaks of **11 Gurus** – the 10 human Gurus plus the Guru Granth Sahib (Sikh Scriptures) which Guru Gobind Singh said would be his successor.

Baisakhi (April) is an important festival celebrating the founding of the **Khalsa** (Sikh fellowship).

The **santoor** is a stringed musical instrument made of wood. It is played by pieces of wood drawn over the strings.

Kirtan is devotional singing which Eeshar would ask God to allow him to take part in at the Golden Temple (Harimandir) in Amritsar (Punjab).

7-11

Eeshar's feelings

- **Proud** – seva, wearing Bana, taking part in Nagar Kirtan
- **Calm and happy inside** – simran
- **Amazed** at Baisakhi story, power of Guru
- **Love** for Gurus expressed in wanting to see them
- **Excitement** prospect of going to Golden Temple
- **Concern** bombings/killings - wanting people to live in peace

I can...

Level 3

- talk about how being a Sikh affects Eeshar's life and describe some of the way his faith makes him feel
- *make links between some of Eeshar's feelings and my own feelings*.

Level 4

- describe some similarities and differences between the things that Eeshar said and how I would have answered the questions
- *describe what or who inspires/influences me and say why*.

See also

Sikh Educational Advisory Services, Guru Guru House, 42 Park Avenue, Crossgates, Leeds, LS15 8EW. Tel: 0113 260 2484. E-mail – khalsafamily@cwctv.net. Roop Singh is a Sikh storyteller for schools. He provides Sikh awareness days, Citizenship days and Indian cultural workshops.

© 2006 RE Today Services
Permission is granted to photocopy this page for use in classroom activities in schools that have purchased this publication.

# Meet Kian

Kian is 10 and lives with his parents and two brothers in Shrewsbury. He belongs to the Bahá'í Faith.

What's the best thing for you about being a Bahá'í?

The best thing is that you get to worship **Bahá'u'lláh** and another thing is that I like to pray with my Dad. At night I pray in my room with my Dad: I put some music on my keyboard and say a prayer; it makes it sound better. I also like the 19-day feasts because all the Bahá'ís get together and I sometimes get to say a prayer in the devotional part or play music.

What would you like to change about your religion?

Nothing. Because I like my religion the way it is and I'm proud of it too.

What is the most special day in your religion?

Well, **Bahá'u'lláh's birthday** (12 November) and **Ayyam-i-Há** (Intercalary Days 26 February – 1 March). On Bahá'u'lláh's birthday it's not just about having a bonfire and eating marshmallows and stuff: it's to celebrate His birth; even though He is already in the next world we still celebrate His birthday, because He is a messenger of God. That's one of the things we believe in our religion. I like Ayyam-i-Há because we have presents and it's a time for thanksgiving.

What is your favourite story from your religion?

The story of Bahá'u'lláh's father's dream, because it's one I know best. In it Bahá'u'lláh's father dreams that his child is a man swimming in the sea and a fish is holding on to each hair of his head, but it doesn't harm Him at all and He is surrounded by light. His father asked a really wise person what the dream meant and he said that it meant that when Bahá'u'lláh grows up everyone would follow and love Him.

Imagine that you could ask God three questions. What would they be?

- What does heaven look like?
- Why did He make stinging nettles? Because they always sting people and they are weeds, or can't they help it?
- I'd like to know what God looks like.

© 2007 RE Today Services
Permission is granted to photocopy this page for use in classroom activities in schools that have purchased this publication.